THE
END
OF
CHILDHOOD

ALSO BY WAYNE MILLER

POETRY COLLECTIONS

We the Jury

Post–

The City, Our City

The Book of Props

Only the Senses Sleep

CO-EDITED BOOKS

Literary Publishing in the Twenty-First Century

Tamura Ryuichi: On the Life & Work of a 20th Century Master

New European Poets

CO-TRANSLATIONS

Zodiac, by Moikom Zeqo

I Don't Believe in Ghosts, by Moikom Zeqo

THE
END
OF
CHILDHOOD

POEMS

WAYNE MILLER

MILKWEED EDITIONS

Published 2025 by Milkweed Editions
Printed in Canada
Cover design by adam b. bohannon
Cover photo by Julie Blackmon
Author photo by Chris Kannen
25 26 27 28 29   5 4 3 2 1
First Edition

LIBRARY OF CONGRESS CATALOGING-IN-PUBLICATION DATA

Names: Miller, Wayne, 1976- author.
Title: The end of childhood : poems / Wayne Miller.
Description: First edition. | Minneapolis, Minnesota : Milkweed Editions, 2025. | Summary: "A tender and provocative collection of poems interrogating the troubles and wonders of both childhood and parenthood against the backdrop of global violence"-- Provided by publisher.
Identifiers: LCCN 2024049489 (print) | LCCN 2024049490 (ebook) | ISBN 9781571315663 (paperback) | ISBN 9781571317902 (ebook)
Subjects: LCGFT: Poetry.
Classification: LCC PS3613.I56245 E53 2025 (print) | LCC PS3613.I56245 (ebook) | DDC 811/.6--dc23/eng/20241023
LC record available at https://lccn.loc.gov/2024049489
LC ebook record available at https://lccn.loc.gov/2024049490

Milkweed Editions is committed to ecological stewardship. We strive to align our book production practices with this principle, and to reduce the impact of our operations in the environment. We are a member of the Green Press Initiative, a nonprofit coalition of publishers, manufacturers, and authors working to protect the world's endangered forests and conserve natural resources. *The End of Childhood* was printed on acid-free 100% postconsumer-waste paper by Friesens Corporation.

For my children, of course

and also for Kevin

after more than two decades
of poetry and friendship

CONTENTS

Toward a Unified Theory   1

———

The Late Cold War   25

In My Country   27

Two Men Shouting   29

On Violence   31

American Domestic   37

Socialist Realism   39

———

On Aesthetics   45

For Sean   49

Texel, 1795   51

Late Capitalism   54

The Trucks   55

The End of Childhood   57

———

On History   61

The End of Childhood   64

Anchorage   66

Thaw 68

Canonical 70

Camoufleurs 72

———

On Narrative 81

What I Know About Tirana 87

Hospital 89

The End of Childhood 91

Belfast 93

On Childhood 96

Notes 101

Acknowledgments 103

It should be possible to build a pagoda of crispbread.

MAX FRISCH

THE
END
OF
CHILDHOOD

TOWARD A UNIFIED THEORY

CHILDREN

Condemned to live

inside the weather
of our moods

JOY

What are you doing?

Filling this bucket with water
and dumping it into the water

1

DEATH

We close their eyes

not for them
but for us

HISTORY

They can't excavate the amphitheater farther

because it extends back
beneath the houses

POETRY

One mouth moving
another

ZOO

The plexiglass
separating us from the animals

brings them closer

FRIENDSHIP

In the instant we both blink
we're blind to each other

it doesn't matter

PANDEMIC

We live inside each other's breath

HISTORY

The man in the grocery store
wearing an ankle monitor—

tube sock pulled up over it

MYTH

Cyclops—
who must wander the earth

with an I in his head

MEMORY

His suffering inside that house

became
the house

PANDEMIC

My son's recurring dream:

sailing a balloon
over an endless ocean

THE FUTURE

Our dead are approaching—
how should we

prepare for their arrival?

MYTH

Whose?

POLITICS

When the plane is going down
all you can do

is hold on
to the thing that's falling

SPOLIA

Gravestones became the walls
of the city, then

the walls
of the houses

DEATH

As a pepper grows
so does the air inside it

ANATOMY LAB

It wasn't that she saw herself
in that grayed entanglement—

She saw no one

POETRY

What are you doing?

Filling this bucket with water
and dumping it into the water

JOY

Those heavy marks in the grass
left by the carnival—

the weight of which
we never considered

not once

MEMORY

Whose?

CATARACT

Between the mind and the page—
the body

CHILDREN

For whom each *species* is a character

FAITH

After his daughter died

he came at last
to believe in God

so he had something permanent

against which
to direct his rage

LOVE

When I was four time zones away from you

I never reset my watch

REVOLUTION

And yet?

Stet.

ROMANTICISM

O luna moth—
born without a mouth!

CATARACT

This eye is still my eye

with a little corporate-made lens
gripped inside it

ELEGY

On her last visit to the mountains
her window
opened onto a stream—

so comforting, she said, to sleep

beside that forever
sound of leaving

LOVE

We live inside each other's breath

EXILE

They built their houses
from the timbers of their ships

DOOR

Means a wall can be broken

and can heal

FIRE DIVER

It's not passing through the fire
you worry about

it's resurfacing

MORTALITY

In your Zoom window
the daylight was rapidly diminishing

Here it was noon

GHOSTS

Whose?

AUDIENCE

Your death became a kind
of microphone

HOPE

In the middle of the drought
the white noise machine

filled our room
with rain

MARRIAGE

And yet?

Stet.

HISTORY

Condemned to live
inside the weather

of our moods

POLITICS

It's good to say:
if the plane goes down

the pilots do too

LANGUAGE

In which death can be
possessed

LITERATURE

Below the flat surface
of the flood:

the city

HISTORY

What are you doing?

*Filling this bucket with water
and dumping it into the water*

———

THE LATE COLD WAR

Children, what can I tell you about that time?

When my parents separated, my father
moved into the college dorms on Jefferson.

I have no idea how this happened.
The adult world was a ceiling of clouds above me.

I saw my father on Saturdays. Each visit
a toy dropped into my hands. Meanwhile

my mother lived on the money her parents gave her.
My best friend's older brother had posters

of nuclear explosions all over his bedroom.
At night they became the walls of his sleep.

He let us listen to Bauhaus and the Damned
until he went to his job at Friendly's

where he sold pot out the walk-up window.
It's impossible to understand what you're born into

until enough time passes that all of it
has been replaced by narrative. One night

we were driving to my father's new apartment
with the woman he'd left my mother for,

and I could see the pale discs of Klieg lights
sweeping across the clouds. I was eight

and terrified the Soviets were invading.
I clutched my backpack full of clothes

in the empty dark of the back seat.
My father, in a moment of pity, assured me

we would drive until we found the source.
It was a car lot having a sale.

IN MY COUNTRY

Mass graves outside the city
Long straight trenches
Industrially made

Caskets lined up perfectly
·Like xylophone keys

A squat yellow bulldozer
Waiting to darken them over
(Drone like a poet
Lifting this image
Into its brain)

Snowfields unraveling
Into streams dark rivers
Cutting the prairie
The voiceless natural world

Foxes in the meadows
Coyotes in the alleys
I keep moving through
My tunnels in the air

I'm in the kitchen for water
Three in the morning

My neighbor's radio
Spilling news across the yard

In the terrarium light
Of the ICU
Sick beds
Lined up perfectly

Music is what I think of
When I encounter such order

The machines breathing
Lifting and falling
Is the music of the State

TWO MEN SHOUTING

The space between them
is a solid object

they push against.

———

I want to make them into a form—

a mirroring—
mouths open,

the mists of their spit
becoming one mist. Their lives

have fallen away,
they are just

this shouting.

———

When they quiet
for a moment

they're like two
balancing

pans of a scale. Then
they lift themselves again

above the room,
where the rest of us

are clearing the table.

————

A ritual of power,
you say,

the structure that holds us—until
one of them

hits the other in the face
with a bottle.

ON VIOLENCE

1

Up on 29th Avenue
a teenage boy was shot

just standing for the bus. All day,
he'd been advancing

toward that bus stop—
as was the bullet, cool and lying

Pez-like in its stack. Blunt metal
driven through his chest

and into the bulletin
board of the air behind him—

every time we walk over
to the ice cream shop

his shadow's pinned there.

2

The panel on the ethics
of violence in literature began

by asking if purely to imagine
a violent act might constitute

an unethical violence
of thought. The answer

was yes—because
to say so allowed the panelists

to flash brightly inside
the airless cavern

of the Marriott. One panelist
suggested that *language*

itself is violence, noting
from his position on the dais

the cruelties of hierarchy.
A question from the audience

employed the image
of *the gel plate of the mind*—

which might have been
the height of the afternoon.

3

Our neighborhood was built
on land that once contained

a creek—and though that creek
has been erased, a heavy rain

will draw a zigzag river
down twelve blocks of streets

and into the open mouth
of the grates on MLK. From there

the water disappears
into the vast system of erasure

that lies beneath this system
of construction we inhabit.

4

In 1917 my great-grandfather
was shot on the stoop

of his rowhouse after a brief
and failed foray into crime.

My grandfather—just a boy—
discovered his father's body,

the trauma of which is why,
my grandmother would say,

he never aspired to more
than basic, menial work.

My grandmother's father
drowned in Sheepshead Bay

after a night of heavy drinking
with the fishermen

he so admired. Foul play
was suspected, but never proved.

This was in 1920. *Back then*,
my grandmother told me,

*things like that happened
all the time.*

5

In 2006 a student
in my composition class

informed me he had no
opinion, story, or thought

worth asserting. He was just
out of the Army

and didn't want to construct
an argument

for my pointless, required course.
He was from a small town,

had only been a nurse
in the war, hadn't seen

anything worth arguing
for or against, hadn't seen

combat—those fifteen months
he'd only been a nurse

in Abu Ghraib.

6

There are two choices:
to bury violence in language

or else, simply, to bury it.
Neither choice is ethical.

AMERICAN DOMESTIC

The drone was *ours*
Slipping home
Toward a distant strip of earth
That was also America

While the operator
Stared into his net of pixels
Then stepped down
From the consequence of the mission
Into the dark grass

Drove the long way
Through the night air
He had to cut
With the blade of his headlights

His family waiting
Behind the heavy curtains
Of that home he'd carried with him
To work and back
As most of us do

Home that fell away
At the required moment

So he could get on with it
What do we say

When he opens the front door
And that bright interior
Flashes suddenly
Into the world

SOCIALIST REALISM

(Tirana, 2019)

In a courtyard behind the museum
stood two derelict statues of Stalin—
each twice as tall as a man,
patinated green, the bases
still slick with last night's rain.

The space was empty except
for two kids rasping up and down
the concrete on skateboards,
then landing with that
familiar, wooden clatter.

One statue's arm had been torn off,
so I could see into the hollow
I imagined was still filled
with the air of the twentieth century.
Inside the museum, the exhibit

was on socialist realism,
because thirty years had passed
and those paintings were now
powerless artifacts—it was
time to consider them

through the abstracting lenses
of period and style. Back home
across the ocean my children
were sleeping, their sound machines
projecting up into their rooms

like statueless plinths. In *Candide*,
the deposed kings will dine forever
in Venice, while all the buoyant,
resolute people in those paintings
are building a future.

They're mortaring walls
and climbing telephone poles,
they're working the fields
in flowery dresses, melting down
metal for I beams and monuments.

The future is *right there*—
a transit station waiting for them
to lock into it. I can't help
but exude my country's aging
narratives of triumph. Art

is not just agreement
or disagreement, you said,
it shapes the moment into form.
In the cab to the airport,
as we slid beneath a dappled

canopy of beeches, the driver
blessed me three times simply
for being an American
who could say in his language
that his country is beautiful.

ON AESTHETICS

Here the boy is fifteen

when his father's friend Paul—
six foot six and seething

because his music career
ended twenty-five years ago

and, ever since, he's taught
middle school—calls the boy

a little prick, a little piece of shit,
because Paul has tried

to play a Stan Getz album
for the boy, and the boy

has looked bored after saying
something vague about

the prog bands he likes,
and so Paul rises, rocking

with the ocean of anger
inside him, and tells

the boy—that little shit—
to stand up and face him—

and the men have been drinking
on the deck for four hours,

and the boy is terrified,
and then the boy's father,

a foot smaller than Paul,
lurches into the man's bulk

and tells him not ever
to fucking talk to his son

like that, not ever, and Paul
says the boy's a little shit

but OK OK take it easy,
and steps back and, sorry,

and now the father is pacing
around the apartment,

caught up in the language
still surging inside him when

he falls against the table,
scudding it across the floor,

and Paul and the boy rush over
to lift the father and carry him

to Paul's bedroom
and lay him down slurring

unintelligibly, and the boy
is frantic because maybe

his father is having a stroke,
a heart attack, but Paul

goes into the kitchen
saying not to worry, he's seen

this sort of thing before,
and holds up the half-empty

fifth the father has chugged
to muster the courage

to stand up to his friend,
and this is where the boy

wants out, wants to leave,
but there's no place to go,

he's caught inside this space,
Stan Getz still playing,

Paul's saxophone case open,
the boy notices, beside the table,

and I think this is too much
narrative, too much play-by-play,

which is why I've given up
every time I've tried to write it

these past fifteen years—
since before my father died—

but now distance
provides a useful objectivity,

so when I watch the boy
lie down beside his father,

finally, in Paul's bed
I can see the darkness

around them for what it is—
shared breath,

which is what this poem
is made of.

FOR SEAN

When I was a boy
I was so often on a plane

in the empty sky
between my parents
in the indistinct care
of flight attendants

that when I handed you
over to the system
of the hospital
it felt like I
had put you on a plane

I imagined you
watching a screen
watching the clouds
the nation below
like a pincushion

where were you going
in that thin bright air
I walked to the vending machines
they were a dark
kind of center

the smallness I was
in those hours
was what I'd thought
my parents became
when I was gone

I tried to read
in my vinyl chair
while you were there
in that parentless place

but also inside
this bit of my childhood

which couldn't protect you
but could
carry you back to me
like a plane

TEXEL, 1795

As the War of the First Coalition closed in the Low Countries,
nineteen Dutch ships sat trapped in ice between Texel and Den Helder.

At dawn, French Hussars charged across the ice pack
and captured the ships without a shot. This is the only time
in recorded history that a cavalry defeated a navy.

I love this story!—the horses' hooves wrapped in muffling cloth,
the ships unable to turn to aim their cannon,
and, of course: the soldiers galloping over deep water.

———

The most famous depiction of Texel is a painting
by Charles Louis Mozin—made in 1836 when the image
of French horsemen crushing a Dutch fleet had clear, nationalistic value.

The only eyewitness account appeared in a newspaper in 1846—
written by a Louis-Joseph Lahure,
who had led the Hussars and now was 79.

Today, Texel is disputed as jingoist propaganda—meant to lift
a nation in decline and to seal in public memory
the name of a dying man.

———

I visited Texel with my half-sister, who married a Dutchman
    in 1991.
We took the ferry across the Marsdiep and to our left was
    Noorderhaaks—
a sandbar island that moves 100 meters every year.

Our father's death hung between us, though we didn't mention it.
I had been close with him; she hadn't spoken to him
for more than a decade before he died.

I think we both were right.

———

Is that true? my children ask, as the narratives
that make the world around them harden into focus.
(What is true? The shifting sea.)

Where exactly were the ships, I said, and Alison pointed
toward the empty air above the water—*About there, I think.*
This made it true.
                    After the surrender,

they must have sat frozen in the ice for many days.
Nothing for the crews to do but stay warm in the dim aftermaths
of those hulls, fixed in place like a story.
I imagine them reading to each other by candlelight—

until, at last, the cold lifted, and the ice broke apart,
and one day all that language
sailed simply back to port.

LATE CAPITALISM

The poets lived their lives
in late capitalism. They wrote their poems, bought their hybrids
in late capitalism. They sent their kids to the best schools they
    could afford
in late capitalism, made their homes in the economic centers
of late capitalism. They pursued each other with the sexual vigor
of late capitalism. They ate the charcuterie platters
of late capitalism. They celebrated the cultural inclusivity
of late capitalism as they taught in the universities
of late capitalism, visited the resort towns
of late capitalism. They rode around the world on the wings
of late capitalism. They retired inside the 403(b)s
of late capitalism. They promoted their events online
in late capitalism. They vaped in the alleys
of late capitalism, drank the imported whiskies
of late capitalism. They gathered conspicuously on the steps
of late capitalism, their meager crowd shook its fists
at late capitalism. They were buried in the caskets
of late capitalism, cremated in the fires
of late capitalism. And you in the future
of late capitalism, looking back at us through the glacier
of late capitalism, what particles do you find sealed
in late capitalism, what light penetrates the glassy compression
of late capitalism?

THE TRUCKS

When the trucks no longer
carried bodies

they carried deodorant
Christmas trees
scented candles
sides of beef

cigarettes honeybees
eye shadow
cheap perfume

they carried microchips
chicken parts prosthetic
joints spiral hams

condoms avocadoes
almond butter
vats of pills

they carried snow
accumulating
in a foreign square
the sensation
of diving into water

voices shuttling
across a table
a galaxy of traffic noise
arriving and arriving

into the economy
we floated on
the trucks were floating

sealing the open
mouths of docks
cut in the walls
at the back of town

they pulled away
full of cargo
wrapped and shut
and carefully tracked

we couldn't wait
to unload them

THE END OF CHILDHOOD

My daughter is building a path
across the lake.

Each morning she goes out
with an armful of boards

and hammers them
into the ice. Her brother

brings the coffee can
of nails, tucks the hammer

into his belt. The ice is thick,
the path is growing.

We watch them
all day from the railing.

No one else lives
at this end of the valley

though up around the bend
there are lights.

My daughter's project
is not to reach them,

she tells us, but just
to leave a perfect

track of boards
floating on the water

that first day
the ice has melted.

———————

ON HISTORY

1

His father's boss was a Millerite—
assured of the imminent apocalypse—

which is how Peter and his parents
came to be among the crowd

that day on Brighton Hill
waiting to be lifted to God

and into the clarity of *story*.
They stayed all afternoon,

small flights of birds
passing overhead. Mr. Jackson

kept saying *soon*, but by nightfall
the oat cakes and lemonade

were gone, and hunger
had become a weight

that could no longer be ignored.
This was the afterlife

they were lifted into: Peter's father
left the factory for another job,

they moved across the river.
The narrow moment of that day

kept swinging like a pendulum—

2

Last week, a violent mob
of thousands stormed the Capitol.

They wore sweatpants and flags,
puffer coats and tactical gear.

If I ignore the details of their chants
and the silliness of their face paint,

they become a historical form.
That policeman on the television

being crushed in a doorway
over and over is trapped inside

of history. If you feel nothing
for him, then you are inhuman.

Yet all of us were pushing
from one side or the other.

3

Peter—that boy I read about
in a book on the history of Cincinnati—

came to see October 22, 1844,
as proof of his parents' incurable

weakness. They, meanwhile,
believed the rest of their lives

to be an enduring humiliation—
how could they have been so foolish?

And yet: many others
made of the experience a church.

The cathedral hung suspended
From the narrow parachute
Of its cupola

That had unfurled
And snapped full with the silent air
Of the thirteenth century

Then I was inside it
Eight hundred years later

The relics I'd read about

Were an ampule of dried blood
And a severed tongue

Pieces preserved in a museum
Pull away from the public
As time passes

But these objects were still
Grotesquely present

Their simultaneous
Persistence and decay

In the packed café across the street
I ordered a beer
And lit a cigarette

I was there on a fellowship
Unreachable to my parents
Except by email
Owing nothing to anyone

And my childhood was a room
I could finally exit
I was sure of it

Not this open world
I would keep entering
From a vaulted and echoing
Darkness

Not my wet blood
My living tongue

ANCHORAGE

Nights awake in my father's house—

    his passed-out snoring down the hall,

his new wife having left again for a hotel,

    the world sealed in snow. To love him

and still want to be lifted from there,

    to want to leave and leave

no footprints. And also the curious wish

    that someone might be awake in a window

watching me. This was, I now realize,

    a first longing to be read—though

I had no interest then in poetry,

which can say: *Child, you will be lifted*

from that room; you can see yourself

from every window—

THAW

Snow retreating
to its fundamental places—

the strip along the fence line,
the heavy shadow
of the shed,

our pressurized footsteps
on the walk, the small

blips in the yard
that inexplicably
last. Once,

in Missouri,
I watched a parked car

slide all the way down
a parking lot's incline
on a loosed sheet of ice.

That moment
remains, though the day
that contained it

is gone. The self
is small patches of snow

resting on nothing—
spring all around them.

CANONICAL

The party was impenetrably
loud and in motion.
Later, the rooms thinned.
It started to snow.
A train roared past
like a redaction. The great writer

played his stereo low;
I sat on the couch
between two aging professors
and pretended to know
what he was playing.
It became clear to me

he was as weak
and terrified as anyone.
When finally
it was just the two of us,
he took down a bottle
and offered the spare room.

Now wind drags over
this house he must have left
while I was sleeping—
where I've awakened
to find myself alone
with all his things.

1

In his time among the camoufleurs
in Amiens, André Mare found

a clear utility in art. The decorative
application of cubist principles

obscured objects on the ground
from the new, godlike planes

that could read the world below them.
Mare saw his role as defending

individual lives, inserting his work
between human bodies and the war.

He would have been horrified,
I believe, when Picasso and Stein

saw on the Boulevard Raspail
a camouflaged truck rattling

toward the front and cried out,
"Yes, it is we who made it!"

In his sketchbooks, Mare
drew the men he served with,

increasingly abstracting them
as they vanished. What he preserved

were his private impressions
of their shapes, complicated

by the fictional, inescapable
demands of form.

2

For months I read obsessively
on the camoufleurs of World War I.

I read of Guirand de Scévola,
Guingot, and Foraine; Léger

and Braque; Wilkinson, Lismer,
and Kerr; Thayer and Brush;

Klee, Solomon, and Marc. I was
fascinated by war's transition

from pomp to invisibility,
and how invisibility was studied

to be artistically reproduced.
When my friends and I went out

into the woods with our BB guns,
we wore our fathers' massive

fatigues. We shot each other
from inside our fathers'

narratives. We finally quit
when Travis got hit in the earlobe

and had to remove the bloody
ball with tweezers. Despite

the risk and thrill, what I loved most
was simply hiding, slipping

into the woods' wash of details
and watching the other boys

run past, knowing they couldn't
see me. My protection

was the world. And then
to stand up and reveal myself

when they came shouting
that it was late, let's go home,

and I had been right there
the whole time.

3

Most readers of poetry assume
the poet is the *I*

pressed up inside the page—
that a poem's artifice works

in the service of rendering the poet
more interestingly visible.

But some poets use their art
to obscure themselves, to disappear

behind the details they've gathered
from the world around them.

When I told my wife
I couldn't understand my fascination

with the history of camouflage,
she—who knows how often

I lay hidden inside my childhood,
and who well understands

the protections of artifice—
said, "Really? You have no idea?"

4

After the war, Mare returned
to Paris, where he designed art

deco interiors with Louis Süe.
Despite an exclusive focus

on painting in his last years,
and despite the arguments

of scholar Claire O'Mahony,
by whom I've come to know

many of his biographical details,
Mare is mostly considered

a minor artist—remembered
for his contributions to the war

and his sleek, stylish interiors—
a flash of movement

inside the vast and disruptive
chaos of Modernism.

5

And you: my oldest friend,
with whom I spent my childhood

in those woods,
who suffered unspeakably

in that house you went home to,
whose abuse occurred

behind a screen
none of us could see through—

after you made clear
how I, too, had failed to see you,

you walked out into the world
and disappeared.

ON NARRATIVE

1

We were in a little beachfront restaurant
when lightning struck a man

maybe thirty feet away
rushing for shelter from the sudden storm

a whiteout explosion the shock
poured down through him

and into the sand
then rose up through the bodies

of his four friends
and they all collapsed

and were dragged inside
what I've learned are *lichtenberg figures*

surfacing on their chests
as the man struck through the head

was given CPR
his body jiggling mute and pale

and our son closed his eyes
against my shirt and you tried

to narrate gently what was happening
and our daughter cried

and that evening the news told us
the man had died

while his friends were *in stable condition*
so when the kids went to bed

at last we drank rum
and said repeatedly in different ways

what had happened

2

It's crass to admit because a man
is dead and my children

are still terrified of thunderstorms
but I know the strange

intensity of this story
and even as I try to honor

the awfulness of the event
the loss of life and its effect

on all of us who were there
in its telling

the story becomes a kind of *pleasure*
if that's the right word

I hate to say it *pleasure*

3

My friend's husband died
quietly after a yearlong fight

with the cancer that had surfaced
inside him

so we attended to her
for a while then left her

swaddled in elegy
and then it was a month

before I saw her again
surprisingly at my local bookshop

laughing with a friend I didn't know
and I'm ashamed to say

I felt in that moment
that she had betrayed her narrative

without permission from those of us
who'd tended that narrative

she'd become a story of pleasure
which was forbidden to her

it was only a momentary feeling
thank god but it happened

so I'm telling you

4

When I think of lightning
pulsing down through a man

then rising up from the ground
into the bodies of his friends

when I think of cancer
dispatching its terrible colonial ships

into new regions of the body
when I think about a story

spreading outward from its event
I think of how aspens

my favorite trees
send up suckers from their roots

that have unfurled
like lichtenberg figures

invisibly beneath the lawn
and this sudden overlay of images

is what became this poem

5

Literature mostly wants the world
to be complex intensified

an entanglement of difficulty
paradox and time

narrowed and compressed
through the strange and disorienting

periscope of the mind
but tonight we'll have a drink together

while the kids watch their show
maybe we'll split a cigarette

out behind our grove of aspens
keeping alive this one

small illicit pleasure
the tiny glowing dot of us

increasing and diminishing
for no one to see

this joy
that's barely worth saying

WHAT I KNOW ABOUT TIRANA

Tirana is a heavy disc of silence
slipped between the mountains and the sea.
Beneath that silence:

thumbing car horns, particles
of language sailing on the air.
In the towering trees

above the Lana River, a cloud
of chirping so dense its outline
can almost be traced in the waxy green.

The children in the schoolyard
are a wellspring of sound,
and in the museum

a swallow trapped in the upper gallery
circles around the room
as if on a string. What else?

The muezzin's call
is light glinting off a needle. What else?
Inside the chess box of this poem,

old men are walking arm-in-arm
across a square, the medieval castle
has grown luminous

with shopping. What else?
The city has slipped again beneath itself.
What else? A travel poem

is like a discharged patient
recalling the time he spent with nurses—
their voices that brushed

against him for simple things,
having covered such a distance
just to cross the room.

HOSPITAL

All the people with their narratives
tucked inside them

like glimpsing out an airplane window

other planes flying

———

I walked the grounds

noting the transitions from grass to concrete
to grass again

I went to the cafeteria

———

I was still inside my body
with its hunger

———

I couldn't decide
if they had turned off a light

inside you

or turned you off
inside the light

———

My mind was just starting to make
the incision

of these words

———

When the text came

I climbed the stairs to find you
inside your body

where you still are

THE END OF CHILDHOOD

(In early B-1 bomber prototypes,
the entire cockpit ejected from the plane . . .)

The thrust of the engines,
the passage of air lifting the wings—

then the cockpit firing violently
upward, the rest of the plane hurtling
beyond us, our parachute opening
to become a little cupola—

and then our falling away
from that lost trajectory, the air
outside the windscreen
gone thick

as we descended through
a sort of chimney in the sky.
We were still strapped inside
the same tight container

that had been the center
of a blue and vast blurring
and now was lying silent
in an empty, furrowed field.

What first arrived was the shock
of our motionlessness,
then a rapid incursion of air
when we opened the hatch.

Then a stranger progressing
steadily toward us—
and the realization
that when he asked if we were OK

we would have to speak.

BELFAST

1

For a while our time there
still fit inside

the narrow lamplight
of the present—not yet memory

but an active location
within the lit circle

we continued
to inhabit. Then

the time began to pull away
like a bead of liquid

holding inside it
my daughter's

voice at that age, the cigarettes
her mother and I

smoked by the stove
once she slept,

the mullioned windows
fogged over for days

so that everything
beyond those rooms

was only a backlit smear,
and the apartment

became sealed and complete—
and we are *here*.

2

I was walking on Corn Market
behind a man

who from my angle
looked exactly

like you (but I was in Belfast;
you were dead).

I held in my gaze
the back of his head,

his shoulders, his lumbering
gait like yours

for two full blocks
and I could almost make it

feel like you and I
were out for a walk

together again.
A slight sensation

of vertigo
and a stolen sort of pleasure

filled me, until
he turned around

to look behind him.

ON CHILDHOOD

1

My daughter has slid down in the bath

so that just the island of her face
breaks the surface—

and when she holds in her breath
her body suspends
touching nothing

I say can you hear me
and she nods from her distance

I say are you ready to come out—
Not yet

2

Inside this larger world
the world of children

is one of such rapidly
shifting allegiances—

now: the adorable predators
now: the adorable prey

3

My childhood became in the end
not a coherent narrative

or even really
a series of flashing images

but simply a feeling—
as though all that time

is a bolt of material
sunk in a basin of dye

4

Childhood is not

as I had thought
the thicket of light back at the entrance

but the wind still blowing
invisibly toward me

through it

5

My children: an encompassing wall
I cannot see over—

such a cramped vantage—

and if that wall collapsed
it would reach out beyond itself

to cover everything

6

In a small train station
in a foreign country

I sat in a molded plastic chair
watching my son

expand his loops
of exploration—

he found a locked door
halfway up the narrow hall

and such was his ignorance

of my place in the world
that he came back

and asked for my keys

Epigraph: Max Frisch, *Man in the Holocene*, translated by Geoffrey Skelton.

"On History": Millerism was a widespread nineteenth-century apocalyptic movement founded by William Miller in upstate New York. When in 1844 Miller's predicted apocalypse failed to occur, the movement evolved into the Seventh-day Adventist Church.

ACKNOWLEDGMENTS

Thank you to the editors of the following publications, where these poems previously appeared (sometimes with different titles and/or in earlier versions):

American Poetry Review: "Toward a Unified Theory"
Anacapa Review: "For Sean"
The Cincinnati Review: "On Narrative"
Cultural Daily: "The End of Childhood [The cathedral hung suspended]," "Socialist Realism"
Divagations: "The Late Cold War"
Dusie [Canada]: "What I Know About Tirana"
The Harvard Advocate: "Canonical"
The Laurel Review: "Texel, 1795"
The Literary Review: "On Aesthetics," "On Childhood"
New England Review: "Camoufleurs"
On the Seawall: "In My Country," "The Trucks"
Plume: "On History"
Poetry: "The End of Childhood [My daughter is building a path]"
Pushcart Prize XLVIII: Best of the Small Presses: "Toward a Unified Theory"
Smartish Pace: "Belfast," "What I Know About Tirana"
Southern Indiana Review: "Hospital"
The Southern Review: "Thaw"

Subtropics: "American Domestic," "Late Capitalism," "On Violence"

32 Poems: "Anchorage," "The End of Childhood [The thrust of the engines]"

Verse Daily: "Anchorage," "Hospital"

Washington Square Review: "Two Men Shouting"

Thank you to Daniel Slager and the rest of the wonderful people at Milkweed Editions.

Thank you to Kevin Prufer, Michael Bazzett, Hadara Bar-Nadav, and Randall Mann for their invaluable edits, advice, and support.

Thank you to the University of Colorado Denver, and thank you to my incredible colleagues—particularly Brian Barker, Nicky Beer, and Joanna Luloff.

Thank you to Rick Barot, Dan Beachy-Quick, Beth Bingham, Justin Boening, Don Bogen, Victoria Chang, Martha Collins, Stephen Connolly, David J. Daniels, Kathy Fagan, Blas Falconer, Piotr Florczyk, Graham Foust, John Gallaher, Sean Hill, Henry Israeli, Ben Johnson, Steven Kleinman, Ada Limón, Adrian Matejka, Erika Meitner, Juan Morales, Manuela Moser, Emily Pérez, Paul Perry, Chris Santiago, Martha Serpas, Stephen Sexton, and Devon Walker-Figueroa—all essential fellow travelers.

Thank you to Jeanne, Harper, and Sean: my world, as ever.

Wayne Miller's books of poetry include *Only the Senses Sleep*; *The Book of Props*; *The City, Our City*; *Post-*; and *We the Jury*. His awards include the UNT Rilke Prize, two Colorado Book Awards, an NEA Translation Fellowship, six individual awards from the Poetry Society of America, and a Fulbright Distinguished Scholarship to Northern Ireland. He has co-translated two books from Albanian—most recently Moikom Zeqo's *Zodiac*, shortlisted for the PEN Center USA Award in Translation—and has co-edited three books, most recently *Literary Publishing in the Twenty-First Century*. He lives in Denver, where he co-directs the Unsung Masters Series, teaches at the University of Colorado Denver, and edits *Copper Nickel*.

milkweed
EDITIONS

Founded as a nonprofit organization in 1980, Milkweed Editions is an independent publisher. Our mission is to identify, nurture, and publish transformative literature, and build an engaged community around it.

We are based in Bdé Óta Othúŋwe (Minneapolis) in Mní Sota Makhóčhe (Minnesota), the traditional homeland of the Dakhóta and Anishinaabe (Ojibwe) people and current home to many thousands of Dakhóta, Ojibwe, and other Indigenous people, including four federally recognized Dakhóta nations and seven federally recognized Ojibwe nations.

We believe all flourishing is mutual, and we envision a future in which all can thrive. Realizing such a vision requires reflection on historical legacies and engagement with current realities. We humbly encourage readers to do the same.

milkweed.org

Milkweed Editions, an independent nonprofit literary publisher, gratefully acknowledges sustaining support from our board of directors, the McKnight Foundation, the National Endowment for the Arts, and many generous contributions from foundations, corporations, and thousands of individuals —our readers. This activity is made possible by the voters of Minnesota through a Minnesota State Arts Board Operating Support grant, thanks to a legislative appropriation from the Arts and Cultural Heritage Fund.

Interior design by adam b. bohannon
Typeset in Adobe Caslon

Adobe Caslon Pro was created by Carol Twombly
for Adobe Systems in 1990. Her design was inspired by
the family of typefaces cut by the celebrated engraver
William Caslon I, whose family foundry served
England with clean, elegant type from the early
Enlightenment through the turn of the
twentieth century.